C0-AWE-316

OUR STUNNING HARVEST

OUR STUNNING HARVEST

Poems

• • •

by

ELLEN BASS

foreword by
Florence Howe

new society publishers

ISBN: 0-86571-052-X Hardbound
0-86571-053-8 Paperbound
Printed in the United States

Cover design by Mara Loft
Book design adapted from a design by Felicia Rice,
Moving Parts Press

New Society Publishers is a project of New Society Educational Foundation, and a collective of Movement for a New Society. New Society Educational Foundation is a nonprofit, tax-exempt foundation. Tax deductible contributions can be made to any of their projects by writing to New Society Educational Foundation, 4722 Baltimore Avenue, Philadelphia, PA 19143. Movement for a New Society is a network of small groups and individuals working for fundamental social change through nonviolent action. To learn more about MNS, write: Movement for a New Society, 4722 Baltimore Avenue, Philadelphia, PA 19143. The opinions expressed in this book do not necessarily represent agreed-upon positions of either of these organizations.

Some of these poems were originally published in the following journals and anthologies: *The Association for Humanistic Psychology Newsletter*, *Calyx*, *Chrysalis*, *Fireweed*, *Frontiers*, *Journal of Humanistic Psychology*, *Matrix*, *Moonjuice*, *Peacemaker*, *Radical Teacher*, *Resource Center for Nonviolence Newsletter*, *Reweaving the Web of Life; Feminism and Nonviolence*, *The Second Wave*, *Sinister Wisdom*, *The Tehachapi Review*, *WIN Magazine*, *Women's Studies Newsletter*.

Ten poems from this book were first published as *For Earthly Survival* in a letterpress edition, designed and printed by Felicia Rice at Moving Parts Press, Santa Cruz, California.

Fire, Seeding Young Groves

Seventeen years ago Ellen Bass was my student, and I was reading aloud to her class "Life at War," a poem that represents Denise Levertov's coming to maturity as a "public poet," as a woman who wrote a great anti-war poem. We were not "feminists" in those days, and the separate pride about femaleness was not part of the emotion we were feeling. But we knew that this poem was special for us: we knew it had come, not out of "gangbusters," but out of an apprehension of intimacy with young and fragile and valued life. We knew it had come also from a sense of the beauty and pleasure of life, and especially of the joy of creation. Today, nearly two decades of the women's movement later, I know that the sense of creation, that intimate sense of connection with new, young life that some women are fortunate to experience, provides special energy and often joy, even to those most oppressed by circumstances.

I don't remember Ellen's reaction that day. I barely remember the class as a group. But I do remember the effort it took to read that poem in my usual composed manner, cooly to discuss its quality, its texture. Perhaps on that day my voice faltered, perhaps a vowel trembled, a syllable wavered. Perhaps that is what Ellen took away with her. Perhaps. For her own poems take risks I would never take, have never taken in my own writing, even privately.

Ellen Bass takes risks in form; she takes risks in content. Even in her earliest published volume eleven years ago, she included a page of prose, and other prose extracts from a Japanese journal, and from the first she wrote freely about sexuality. Why not? The wonder is not appropriate; it is only because Ellen comes from me, my classroom, that I marvel. Poets are supposed to experiment, to dare, to stretch the language in print, not only in their "closets."

Ellen celebrates that particular day in my classroom in a poem addressed to me. She remembers my emotion. She is part of a young generation of women who grew up during the sixties, who remember the civil rights and antiwar movements, and for whom the War in Vietnam was watershed. Young women in Ellen's generation experienced the full force of the feminist movement at the climax of their marriageable and child-bearing years. They are among the first women of any generation to have available to them from the past the rich stream of women writing in their own tradition. The extraordinary poetry—and prose—emerging today from women just forty or a bit younger (consider Alice Walker, Mary Gordon, Susan Griffin) carry that tradition forward.

In the early seventies, Ellen and I coedited a volume of American women poets called NO MORE MASKS! used today in college classrooms. The correspondence of those years—Ellen lived in Boston and I in New York—includes her response to my request for some of her poems. She sends me five, and adds, "If I look like a pig I'll look like a pig. This is the hardest way to get published I know. It's like being the editor of *The Atlantic* for 20 yrs. just to get your story in. But I'll stop complaining." Ellen did the drudgery for that volume without much complaining. And when I was not an effective or an efficient collaborator, she wrote so honestly that I had to respond in kind. She came to know a great deal about my life, even about my writing blocks.

Only after the publication of NO MORE MASKS! could either of us care about poetry in a new and special way, acknowledging its relation to our own lives, understanding that if we were to become poets, we were part of a stream of women who had been writing poetry and feeling alien: "We are a queer lot," Amy Lowell wrote in 1925, "We women who write poetry."

In the eleven years since that anthology was published, Ellen and I have corresponded, met occasionally, and loved across the continent. She has continued to send me her poems, and her volumes of poems. In the last five years, I have sent some few poems to her. We have changed places: she is now the published poet, the teacher of other would be poets, and I am the student, the closet poet, the person too shy to show my poems to any one but my former student.

I am pleased to see this new volume begin with a poem that marks Ellen Bass as a teacher, and as the kind of teacher I feel proud to be my "inheritor." She is that, as she defines *her* student's poem as "swimming," as "walking," as "coming home, returning/by a different route," as

> . . . what comes in place of sleep
> what we ask to know
>
> a tribute to redwood pods, they
> burst within fire, seeding
> young groves

New York City, 1984

Contents

for Sara, that she may live to love the earth
and receive her blesssings

Then call it swimming

for Susan Lysik

you are concerned. your writings
are not poems—there are no line breaks
sentences wind like coils of a pot

they are not stories—no beginning
middle, end, characters
are not developed
the action is a child
turning
in green chiffon

you apologize: I
don't know what to call it
you want a name

then call it swimming. the water passes over you
the smoothness
the liquid
the smoothness more enveloping than making love
your arm, arching in the sun
lit drops, crystals, falling

or call it walking, the air
cold in your nostrils
the ground soft with rotting leaves
the green is too bright

some are mushrooms, some maize
some take long as persimmon to fruit
some leave neatly
they are the black pearl droppings of deer
some are overgrown pups
they hang on your tit, you cannot
shake them off

call it
coming home, returning
by a different route

call it a sandwich in waxed paper
we will give it to our children

call it an antidote
to what we have been taught

call it rubble, what remains
through pyres, altars, ovens, electricity

call it what comes in place of sleep
what we ask to know

a tribute to redwood pods, they
burst within fire, seeding
young groves

Creation

for Alan

I bleed at full moon, my blood fruit red in the light.
"Full," you say, "you feel so full."

In Zambesia women bleed together at new moon.
Then at fullness, when light pours in
through openings in their huts, dazzling their eyelids
they release, each, an egg. The moon
calling the egg, calling
the women, the men
to dance, to touch bare feet to glowing earth
to circle, to couple, to conceive.

The moon awakens me, it
strokes me like a lover.
I come on bare feet to your bed.
Full yoni, full lingam, full moon
and my blood flowing, allowing
this ceremony, this prayer
that rain will muddy fields, tulips
open into red feather cups
damp calves suck our fingers.

We rouse the waters with the moon. We leaf
willows, blue herons
nest in them.

Remembering our past

Remembering our past
starts simply. We go back
to our childhood. We write
about the hallway window
that looked into Zoffer's.
Florence Zoffer, she asked my brother
to teach her tennis. She wanted him
for a boyfriend, mother said.
She was too old, had orange hair. I watched her
take off her blouse, hang it in
the closet, her slip.

We go back to our mothers and our fathers.
She was in nurse's training.
Eleven hour shifts.
When he took her to the movies, it was warm, quiet,
she fell asleep. He said
let's go sometime when you're not so tired.
There is no time, she said.

We tell the stories, our
grandmothers, his mother. She was
a pretty woman. When the coal
train went by she
ran outside. They waved
to her and kicked coal off the car.

Our grandmothers, her mother.
I screamed when the train went by.
The noise. The rumble in the floor.
She told me, my boyfriend
is on the train. Come with me, see,
we will wave to him. My boyfriend.
See. We waved.

We go back, her mother was
Sarah, her mother Nochoma.
We start with what we know.
Then we continue—her mother and hers.
Her mother and hers.
We are in Lithuania, Russia.
We are in Poland, Yugoslavia.
We are in Sweden. We are in Ireland.
We are in Puerto Rico. We are in Mexico.

We are in Rome, Greece. We are in
Mesopotamia, Crete. The names
go through their transformations

Sally, Sarah, Sappho, Selene, Ceres
Cybele, Sophia, Athene, Diana
Artemis, Anat, Isis, Ishtar, Astarte, Minerva, Dana
Tiamat, Potnia. Say the words.

Lycia, Athens, Lemnos, Lesbos
Cantatiria, Atlantis, Catal Huyuk
Mycenaeans, Anatolians, Lydia, Caria
Lavinia, Latium, Julia, Claudia, Rhea
Alalakh, Altamira, Anna Nin.
Say the words.
This is the beginning.

Tampons

My periods have changed. It is years
since I have swallowed pink and gray darvons, round
chalky midols from the bottle with the smiling girl.
Now I plan a quiet space,
protect myself those first few days when my uterus lets
go and I am an open anemone. I know
when my flow will come. I watch my mucous pace
changes like a dancer, follow the fall
and rise of my body heat. All this
and yet I never questioned them, those slim white handies.

It took me years to learn to use them
starting with pursettes and a jar of vaseline.
I didn't know where the hole was.
I didn't even know enough
to try to find one. I pushed until
only a little stuck out and hoped
that was far enough.
I tried every month through high school.

And now that I can change it in a moving car—
like Audrey Hepburn changing dresses in the taxi
in the last scene of Breakfast at Tiffany's—
I've got to give them up.

Tampons, I read, are
bleached, are
chemically treated to
compress better,
contain asbestos.
Good old asbestos. Once we learned not to shake it—
Johnson & Johnson's—on our babies or diaphragms,
we thought we had it licked.

So what do we do? They're universal.
Even macrobiotics and lesbian separatists are hooked on them.

Go back to sanitary napkins?
Junior high, double napkins
on the heavy days, walking home damp underpants
chafing thighs. It's been a full twelve years
since I have worn one, since Spain when Marjorie pierced my ears
and I unloaded half a suitcase of the big gauze pads in the hotel trash.

Someone in my workshop suggested tassaways, little
cups that catch the flow.
They've stopped making them,
we're told. Women found they could reuse them
and the company couldn't make enough
money that way. Besides,
the suction pulled the cervix out of shape.

Then diaphragms.
It presses on me, one woman says.
So swollen these days. Too tender.

Menstrual extraction, a young woman says.
I heard about that. Ten minutes
and it's done.
But I do not trust putting tubes into my uterus each month.
We're told everything is safe
in the beginning.

Mosses.
The Indians used mosses.
I live in Aptos. We grow
succulents and pine.
I will buy mosses
when they sell them at the co-op.

Okay. It's like the whole birth control schmeer.
There just isn't a good way. Women bleed.
We bleed.
The blood flows out of us. So we will bleed.
Blood paintings on our thighs, patterns
like river beds, blood on the chairs in
insurance offices, blood on Greyhound buses
and 747's, blood blots, flower forms
on the blue skirts of the stewardesses.
Blood on restaurant floors, supermarket aisles, the steps of government
buildings. Sidewalks

Gretel's bread

will have

like

blood trails,

crumbs. We can always find our way.

We will ease into rhythm together, it happens
when women live closely—African tribes, college sororities—
our blood flowing on the same days. The first day
of our heaviest flow we will gather in Palmer, Massachusetts
on the steps of Tampax, Inc. We'll have a bleed-in.
We'll smear the blood on our faces. Max Factor
will join OB in bankruptcy. The perfume industry
will collapse, who needs
whale sperm, turtle oil, when we have free blood?
For a little while cleaning products will boom,
409, Lysol, Windex. But
the executives will give up. The cleaning woman is leaving a
red wet rivulet, as she scrubs down the previous stains.
It's no use. The men would have to
do it themselves, and that will never come up

for a vote at the Board. Women's clothing manufacturers, fancy
furniture, plush carpet, all will phase out. It's just not
practical. We will live the old ways.

Simple floors, dirt or concrete, can be hosed down
or straw, can be cycled through the compost.
Simple clothes, none in summer. No more swimming pools.
Swim in the river. Yes, swim in the river.
Dogs will fall in love with us.
We'll feed the fish with our blood. Our blood
will neutralize the chemicals and dissolve the old car parts.
Our blood will detoxify the phosphates and the
PCB's. Our blood will feed the depleted soils.
Our blood will water the dry, tired surface of the earth.
We will bleed. We will bleed. We will
bleed until we bathe her in our blood and she turns
slippery new like a baby birthing.

The pigeons

doves or pigeons
in the late afternoon, sun
on their wings
they would circle, dip
gleam white, dark
as they shifted, shadow.

When they flew close, the sound
of their wings, small bodies through air.
The softest
sound, softer
than water.

Watering plants
by the carnations
looking up, the half moon
white in pale sky
birds white
dark, soft as they flew,
I thought of Thoreau
one raining night, how rain
spoke innocently upon ridges.
He would listen, he wrote
he would listen as long as it spoke.

I thought
I would listen to my doves that way, receive them
as long as they circled, shone
white, dark, soft
wave sound of air. But

another day. I
entered the house, began dinner
read perhaps. I don't remember
the next day. The next

they did not come as I did yoga on the porch.
I thought maybe it's too late.
I looked earlier
the next. Tuesday at dinner
a few birds flying by the window, white
underbellies. Look—are they pigeons?
but they were barn swallows, singly
or in two's or three's.

Oh birds,
I want to make you promises
take lover's vows to bring you back.
I think
maybe the moon is too bright for you, maybe
you will return when she wanes again
maybe there is too little water, maybe
too warm, maybe
maybe

To Alan

The earth turns. Trees
are almost to the sun
on our ridge. Clouds
rib the sky.

Small peach-hooded birds flit
to and from their mud nest
in the eaves. Sage grows,
leaves soft and furry
like an animal, smell
strong. It will be good in soup.

I lay in the grass in a gingham dress.
Elastic loose in the waist and sleeves,
they flare like elephant ears.
My ring gleams in the last sun.
This wide ring, the kind I wanted
though I'd been told
women with short fleshy fingers
do not wear wide bands.
You said, "if you want a wide band . . ."

We fought yesterday, eroding
each other like water
through cleancut forest.
When I came home I found your note,
on rice paper, you signed
"your husband." Yes
you are my husband. You
will not leave. And I,
even when I take off my ring,
wear a wide pale band.

Even our language

The word *innocent* means *not guilty*
free from sin, guileless, simple, naive
and *unsullied.*

The dictionary example is *innocent snow.*

They mean snow which hasn't been walked on,
blown gray by car exhaust, turned slush,
been scraped to gutters in unmeltable piles.

Do they think this snow is then guilty?
Has it sinned? Has the snow been
asking for it? Did it have it coming?
Was it out at night? Did it
give in too easy?

Why doesn't the little girl tell
when the dentist or the neighbor or her father
reaches under her skirt and splits
her small opening with a shove?

Why doesn't she tell?

Webster's will tell you:
when you're no longer innocent
you're guilty.

Roget's thesaurus

I am writing a poem about birth
and need an image for *pushing through*
pushing out. Roget's thesaurus lists
push aside, *push back*, *push down*, *push forward*
push in, *push off* and *upon*.
It also considers *push the pencil*, *push car*, *pusher*, and *push-over*.

On page one opposite a sepia portrait
is Roget's biography:
"Peter Mark Roget was the only son of John Roget."
Ah. So there was no *pushing out*.

Let me explain

Let me explain. I was not
violently raped. He was a man, a boy
I knew. We'd been in junior high together,
other boys called him faggot because
he threw like a girl. He got poor grades
but read—more than me—a
book a week. After high school he
joined the Coast Guards, told his girl
it was college. When she found out
she left him. I saw him now and then
on vacations. The summer before
I wore a pair of pale blue shorts.
He took me for a drive, kissed
the inside of my wrist. I was
a virgin. A friend of his once
did it to a virgin and she wouldn't stop bleeding.
We parted chaste. He wrote a few times
from Cambodia, criticized the war protestors, told me *I*
meant well, but those others . . .

When he returned to the States
we bought a bottle of champagne, drank it
sitting in the lifeguard stand, watching the ocean.
He talked and talked, the scorpions,
the whores, the endless nights on watch.
We went for a drive, he parked, and talked,
he talked, the heat, the stench, the
loneliness, the whores, their children whores.
I listened. He talked. And then he wanted,
he wanted. He loved me. He wanted to marry me.
Enter and burrow, soft, warm,
where there were no scorpions, no exploding grenades, no
rotting old men. I was clean.
I was a college girl. I had full breasts
and smelled of Camay.
He was home and it was time.

No, I said. I love someone else, I said. It's
different now, I said. I want to be your friend, I said.
You just want someone smarter than me, he said,
more educated. It's because I haven't been to college.
It's because I'm not a doctor. It's because I'm not rich.
I love someone else, I said.
The whores, he said, like their mothers, the
stench, the rotting old men, the hungry children, I
need you, he said, I need you.
I can't, I said. I won't, I said. I love someone else, I said.
I need you, and the tears, and I need you, as the car filled
with scorpions and whores, grenades, children, rotting men and
I wanted to get home.
I wanted to get away. I would do anything to get away.

Go ahead, I said
and lay down on the front seat,
my head under the steering wheel.
Umph, he groaned, pushing, hey,
are you a virgin? and
came immediately, apologizing.
It didn't take long and
I was home.
He said, I hope you get pregnant, then
you'll have to marry me.
I'm on the pill, I said.
I hope you get pregnant, he said again.

So you see, it was not a violent rape.
I was not afraid for my life.
We drank champagne together.
I lay down myself.

This was the kind of rape
most people don't even call rape.

This was the kind of rape
I didn't know I could refuse.

Weeds

for Alan

"The fire marshal'll be coming by
about all those weeds," a neighbor motioned Alan.
"I'm renting a tractor with a big rototiller.
You want to go in on it?"
"That'll just leave mud," Alan said.
"Only for about a week. Then it'll harden up."
"But then we'll have caked dirt."
"Aw we oughta have another rain or two yet,
so you'll get a little low growth back."

This morning is cool and cloudy.
We woke at seven to the sound of trucks
spraying the apple orchard down the hill.
But in our weeds, our green leafy weeds
that have blossomed yellow and white and lavender,
thick masses of small lavenders,
a flock of tiny red-and-orange-headed birds,
red from their heads down onto their backs,
peck and hop, and a pair of yellow goldfinch
fly from the oak to the blue sierra.

Walk with sunshine

On the way there he doesn't see the cat,
a gray and white tabby curled in the tall grass.
But coming back he pauses, takes sight
and there is nothing I can do to stop him.
They are off across the pasture and the man
stands watching not a hundred feet from me in his yard.
"SUNSHINE!" I yell. "Sunshine come here,"
clapping my hands, the hot afternoon air
thick with the hum of bees, broken by my screams.
"SUNSHINE! SUNSHINE!" I am sweating. "Come here. Come here."

Finally when the cat has eluded him, he comes trotting back
past the cows, through the pasture fence.
"Sit down," I tell him and I smack his head.
"No," I say sternly. "No. No. No."
And smack his head again. "Sit down."
Then I give him a long lecture on how if he continues to chase cats
we won't be able to go on this walk anymore
and with a final smack we rise and turn toward home.

The man is still in his yard.
"I am trying to teach him not to chase cats," I say with a strained smile
hoping he doesn't threaten to shoot Sunshine.
        "Well, that's their life," the man says.
Flustered and still sweating I say, "I'm just afraid he might catch one."
        "He might," the man says.
"But fortunately the cats are faster than he is."
        "I know that," he says gently.

"Thanks," I say and walk on, Sunshine walking ahead.
"Good dog," I say softly to his rump, "good Sunshine."

Was I planned?

Was I planned? you will ask.
Yes, you were planned.
As it was planned that I should meet your father one
October when Boston leaves were the color of rose petals,
that we should find a cottage where the curl
of Cape Cod is no wider than a pasture,
and the sun rose through the ocean and
arced down into the grassy bay with the
ease of something well planned.

And I am a lucky woman

Strawberry red tubers swell from the tips of the cactus
and I am swelling too.
At moments like this when the nausea abates
I splash cool sea water over my head
and every shell I pick up is big enough to hold you,
little scallop, little clam.
Your father made me laugh this morning,
caught me making patterns of the yoghurt in the bottom of my bowl
tears about to salt the ridges.
You are a lucky baby.
He will make you laugh.

The first night we spent in his basement apartment
I put on my nightgown.
He pleaded with me not to sleep in it, but I was cold.
The only heat was from pipes that led to upstairs radiators.
So he put on his father's great coat
with lapels and a big fuzzy collar
and climbed in too.
We were doubled over with the laughter, with the love,
with this life we had stumbled upon.

Your father is a lucky man.
Now that you are coming he no longer thinks he will
die young.
He will live, little walnut,
little walnut with your wavy arms,
he will live to make you laugh.

"I've got to hurry up and go to bed so I can wake up and take a nap" or Sara at six weeks

Other women tell me, "Yes
I felt it too," winding up the baby swing
12 minutes, *Frère Jacques* and the reassuring
slide-click slide-click
the gear going round.
12 minutes, time to shit and shower.
Pit-stop precision. I make dinner one round,
eat the next. If I don't chew
I have time to wash the dishes.

Before she was born I pictured lazy afternoons beneath the oak tree,
long walks, nursing in the sun.

It's hot in the sun. Flies swarm.
There are ants beneath the oak and
mainly we walk the kitchen linoleum.

I am always afraid she's going to cry.
I cry. My shoulders knotted like a girl scout's lanyard,
my right eye twitching like in college when I broke
my engagement and memorized the whole of 19th century English poetry.

And insomnia.
Last night I woke at four while Sara slept on soundlessly.
I nudged Alan, then fought with him, paced
drank tea and took hot showers, till she stirred
and I could hold her, flannel bundle
and be comforted.

Relax, Ellen. Relax.
This fat muffin, this honeysuckle
she is here to pleasure me, she is here
to slow me down.

She will be a baby so briefly,
briefly, almost the day moth.

Already she is pushing up with her feet.
On Monday she struggled, straightening knees
to stand leaning on my breast.
Today is Friday and she does it, even pushes
her body away with her arms.
And grunts, grunts.
I can feel her fly.
Baby
you will fly. I don't want to miss you,
so busy with the twitch in my eye, I never see
your lopsided smiles, changing diapers so fast
I forget to squeeze your sturdy legs,
don't rub my cheek on your belly.

Little buffalo, Saraswati, teach me
slow, oh
teach me slow.

Evening

The sky glows amethyst, the pines
still black forms. I sit with Sara, nursing, as night sifts
and she, like sand through oceans, sifts into deeper sleep.
We have been buying groceries. Milk and eggs are in the icebox.
The rest sits in brown bags.
As windows light in houses, ours stay dark.
Her tiny hand stirs on my belly.
I feel the warmth of her pee, its
musky sweet smell.

There is a woman

There is a woman. She is young.
She pushes her baby in a canvas stroller. Her wavy hair
is only beginning to gray.

Her daughter sucks her fist and coos.
The stroller rumbles over the bumpy asphalt:
the burnt gold skeletons of thistles,
the purple feather weeds, the smell of late summer dust;
soft thud thud of a woodpecker
when she stops to pick blackberries
plump as her baby's thigh.

Even a year ago she would have said how blessed
she felt to have these days, this interlude,
her world spotted giraffes with their delicate horns
and trees with leaves in crayon box colors.

But that time is already past.
She has been storing these years
like plants store sugars in their roots,
like the black earth stores sun,
and her baby stores milk in her wide duck belly for the night.

Later she will cut yellow roses,
set them in water on her husband's desk.
She will dial the phone and take laundry out of the dryer.
And she will struggle with words, with these words
but not with the words, with the meaning
of the words, with the meaning of her
life in a world where the season is closing
and will there be another?
and is there anything that she can do?
and can she do it?
and will she?

They're family men

I say to myself, they're
family men, have children, some
grandchildren. And though they haven't
held their wives as they pushed,
veins strained like April rivers
or carried the newborn while its hairs
held the wet pattern of its birth, still
they must have stood in woolen bathrobes heating bottles
must have rocked the squalling child till it sucked
        and softened into ovaled arms.
Or if not that, they must have once
touched their finger to a cheek, pink
as silkwood blossom, head pussy willow soft,
or seen a mouth open in first smiles,
the tiny point of the gums, the half-a-moon grin,
and the sounds–
they couldn't help hearing the sounds,
the roll of the r's, the gurgle in the bath.

They love their children.
They see they don't have diaper rash,
wear shoes too small or play in the street.
They fasten headlights to their bicycles
and coax them to eat carrots.

Yet they work for Bechtel. They work for Lockheed.
They work at the nuclear power plants at
Hanford, Washington; West Valley, New York.
They dump wastes in the San Francisco Bay.
And they say, "Don't worry."
They say, "It's safe."
They say, "The economy, jobs, and fuel."
And I ask myself, how?
I ask myself how? and what do they
tell themselves?

When they dance at their daughter's wedding,
when they dance at their son's wedding,
when they drink imported champagne and roast beef is
excellent, little ones in party clothes
crawl under linen tablecloths
and even the grandmother two-steps a bit in blue shoes—
at night when they get into bed and kiss their happy wives goodnight,
how? how do they keep from thinking
that their grandchildren will never see grandchildren?

Walk

He carries the child, sweatered and
owl-eyed in the country night.
She pushes the empty stroller, too light
                veering
    like the dog with the metronome tail.

No one speaks.
They are not going anywhere
in particular.

I didn't know

for Florence Howe

Ten years ago I sat in a classroom next to my teacher.
We sat in a circle at half desks. She, on my right
read a poem by Denise Levertov, *Life at War*
and she choked back tears.

I was a beginning poet.
I wrote of love and jacaranda trees.
Once I tried to write about the war,
but the poem was not one that would make anyone
choke back tears.

I wished, as I heard her read, and afterward,
I wished I could write that way
about those things.

I didn't know I would have to
wake with the taste of them thick in my saliva,
to wake with the sweat of them, with low groans,
to hear my husband grind his teeth with dreams of them.

I didn't know I would have visions of my baby's skin
sloughing off from radiation burn,
that in the sweetest times, especially
the sweetest times, pink dusk, my baby sucking,
patting my breast, or after she's in her small wicker bed
when Alan lights orange candles and incense
and we turn to our own loving,
I didn't know I'd come to where there is no joy
without that pale underbelly of what is to come.

I didn't know
what I wished for.

Eat the grouse

"Eat the grouse," my father-in-law tells us
from his hospital bed, needle in vein
yellowed skin below his eyes
but cheeks ruddy. I'd prepared myself for worse
as I cancelled appointments, packed diapers
for the baby, his grandchild—that he should see her.
"Have you ever eaten it?" he asks me, the newcomer,
Eastern Jew whose mother has explained
so we know it by heart, *Jews don't hunt.*
We know what it is to be hunted.

My mother-in-law says, "I just
never get enough of that grouse.
But you got to eat it right away
or it gets tough."

I am a vegetarian.
Not even turkey at Thanksgiving.
But I take three grouse from the freezer
and remind Alan to be on time.
We pray, then eat.
Two small pieces are left over.
I finish them before bed.

The next day Dad is home
making a fire in the basement stove.
He refused their operations,
said he'd take his own chances.

On the weekend, we load the car for the cabin.
"Get my gun," he tells Alan.
"Dad, the doctor said no lifting over five pounds."
"It's not over five pounds," he protests.
"No, but when you shoot the impact's sixty or seventy."
He smiles, "Then you take it. We might see grouse."

Alan and I circle the lake.
He carries the gun.
"Will you mind if I shoot?" he asks.

I think of the clubbing of seals
for their coats, of rabbit feet, snake skin,
the slaughter of buffalo, massive thick hulks, for their tongues.
And the grouse, and the families of grouse.

I think of my father.
He cried in Russian forests,
an infant in his mother's arms
as she travelled by night, hid by day.
She could hear the soldiers' boots pack snow.
They could hear my father's cries above her shushing.
They pretended not to hear.

Alan is telling me stories, his father
and his father's brothers hunted the family meat,
it was what they had.
And when he was young, the two of them sat
dark to dusk in the duck blind,
freezing in drizzle, silent, still.
The men would never lose a cripple,
could follow deer for miles by bits of hair on bushes.

I see Dad back in the cabin.
He built it with another fellow
spring after Alan was born,
carpeted with squares from sample books.
Now there's electricity, but they still
carry water from the lake.

"Not many more duck seasons left in me,"
he's been saying the last couple years

and we'd laugh, "You'll be saying that twenty more."
But now we don't know.
We don't know.
We know only we have this season,
the yellow poplar leaves padding the walks,
wind whipping up off the lake,
Mom wiping out the icebox and grumbling about the time
someone left worms in it all winter,
the baby shaking her lambie by its pink and white ear,
and him, sitting,
this man who never sat before, watching her,
calling her sweetheart.

"When you got me, did you want a boy?"
Alan asked his mother in the car.
"Oh yes," she said. "I wanted the baby for me,
the boy I thought for Dad to teach hunting and fishing,
and then I'd give the man to God."

"'Will you mind if I shoot?" I hear Alan asking.
"No," I say, "No. I don't mind."

Even this

My daughter
is five months old. I take her
with me to a slide presentation.
The room is darkened, she sleeps on a quilt.

The woman's voice is clipped, rushed
as she narrates. She has more facts
than time—
    children in pornographic magazines,
    girls in suggestive advertising,
    in films, child prostitutes,
    children with venereal disease, babies
    three month old babies
    treated in hospitals
    for gonorrhea
    of the throat.

My baby sleeps, sucking
her thumb. When she wakes
she will suck my breast. The instinct
is strong, the muscles of the jaw, strong.
That first week, when my nipples were sore
she sucked my finger, her father's finger.
We laughed, startled by the power of her suck.

She sucks the ear of her rubber cat.
She greets the world with an open mouth.
A baby will suck anything.

November air

November air cool in my throat
and morning sun hot on my back
I walk wheeling Sara. She wears
red overalls and a plaid flannel shirt,
her first time out of pastel.
She coughs and I look down–
she has pulled out her tongue
as far as it will go and is
playing with it.

Along the road are frosted eucalyptus leaves,
soft purple of new acacia stems, the intricate
feathered green. The ground is bumpy with acorns,
smooth shells and stiff burr caps.
Red and yellow apples lie thick under trees
melting down to a dusty sauce,
and in the lupine, birds rattle the dry seed pods
till I hear water, till I hear lake waves.
It is too sweet.
It is too sweet to give this up.

When we flew to Minnesota
Sara fussed and I bounced her endlessly,
tried nursing, singing, the rattle, the teething ring.
I thought, it's not natural to be up here.

> Looking down over the mountains, great madder red slabs,
> the bleached salt flats, tawny plains, and the waters,
> copper sun broken over the waters.

Then the cities, the places where people live,
concrete, steel, and glare
of metal on parked cars.
The building, the building, as if we couldn't
leave anything alone.

When Japanese arrange flowers, the space
between the flowers is considered,
the shape of space between.

But they pave their land as thoroughly,
men pouring asphalt over the world.
While young pines, smooth green stems just beginning to form bark,
bamboo, still thin as flower stalks,
earthworms, their bodies soft and wet as open melons,
these are paved under

until the earth sours, puckers
like skin beneath a cast left on too long;
the oceans, that have born oysters, salmon, whales, kelp,
heave their dead upon the beaches
like drugged women laboring;
the air carries poison, like it once
carried pollen, like it once carried
the smell of quince or of the sea, the air
even where it's innocently clear
harbors a slow betrayal.

We have always had war.
We have always had drought, had famine—
    a mother's hands, the veins risen like mountain ranges,
    that cannot feed her children—
had company towns, had share croppers, had piece work—
    fingers stiff with the factory twist-place, twist-place, twist-place,
    twist-place.
Mothers have worried their
infants to survive the fever,
their sons, the mine,
their daughters, the babies, the beatings.

We have always had
what to worry.
And now, all life is threatened–
    the deer, the gudgeon,
        the wild radish, orchid, cockatoo,
            the walrus, the wasp, the
                very texture of the soil, the solidity of ice caps, the
                    spring thaw.

Mornings I lie in bed,
sun pouring through the window like a fugue,
my feet cold under blankets.
The vastness, the immeasurable
loss thins my blood.

And it if weren't that I had to feed my baby,
and feed the dog, and by then I'm up and might as well
throw in the laundry, get the mail . . .

I pick up Sara, carry her outside
and on the hard dirt behind the house
I see a thin salamander, still, puffing.
There's a whole new crop of them,
and as I bend to look closer,
the sheer web of toes, the membrane
of throat filled round as a cherry,
my hair brushes Sara's face
and she grabs, squealing, stuffing it into her mouth.

For my husband's mother

Those months I carried Sara
I'd think of your mother,
the woman who carried you
though she could not
keep you.
            This woman
we do not know, this girl
whose life was changed
in ways we'll never know,
who wanted or did not want
who loved or did not love
who chose or did not choose
but, willing or reluctant
carried you.

Easily, like the grass that sprouts the pasture green
after first fall rains; or in great pain,
volcanic, slow,
the creaking
cracking of the earth, she
birthed you.

We do not know her name
or what she thought as her fingers soaped her taut
belly in the bath,
as your kicks reached her
first uncertain, then
definite, firm rabbit thumps.

We do not know if she could
keep food down, if
her legs cramped,
if she grew dizzy in the grocery
had to drop her head between her knees
to keep from blacking out.

We do not know if she held you in her hospital bed,
if her breasts were bound to keep the milk from
letting down
or if they drugged her and she woke
only to the new softness of her belly, like dough.

We do not know
what friends or family criticized her, if they
sent her out of town and brought her back
as though she'd been on holiday.

We know only
there was a woman who gave you
the food of her blood
the bed of her flesh,
who breathed for you.

We do not know
if anyone ever
thanked her.

Keeping records

Her Grandmother bought her a baby book
and everyone advised me, write
write it down or you'll forget
how old she was when she first
held her head up, smiled, turned over.

They're right. I will forget.
But I'll remember it was in September,
her hair, blowing in the hot wind
like a young colt's fur, and someone—
Janet—in an old VW, the gas pipe came loose,
we had to stop to reconnect it on the way—
Janet drove us to the beach. It was
the hottest day that summer she was born,
and her hair, her blond hair was like
a colt's mane in the dry wind.

And I'll remember nursing
in the brown stuffed rocker.
Alan asleep, dog asleep,
no shine of car lights on the foggy windows,
no roosters, no baa-ing of the goat.
Only her warmth in my lap, the small sound of milk
squirting inside the tiny cave of her mouth
and her regular gulps. Her hand
plucking the woolen blanket, wandering in air,
then palm and fingertips padded like a kitten paw
she stroked my hand, over
and over.

And she'll remember—the blue
satin ribbon of my nightgown, the slide
of one side, the ridges of the other,
the limp tails of them she bats and sucks.
My sleep smells and milk smells and

my feet clomp clomping to her crib.
She'll remember my clavicle under her forehead
and my hand patting her back to sleep.

And perhaps we'll remember today. The rain
coming down to the earth in great watery profusion,
the metallic thunking in the gutters
and wooden patter on the roof,
drops hanging from the rungs of lawn chairs
like beads of an abacus. She sleeps.
I curl close around myself like a wintering snake.
When she wakes I will go to her.
She will see the white blocks of my teeth,
the white hairs woven into the brown
like threads in a nest. She will hear my murmurs
within the murmur of the rain.
I will see her tongue, softer than peach fruit,
her eyes, open skyward as the mouths of baby birds,
her own mouth spread into a gummy smile.
I will hear her chirps.

Later she will chug across the kitchen linoleum,
hands and knees synchronized,
grunting hah! hah! hah! hah!
wild with her own momentum.

I will not remember what
day this is, what month, her age.
But I will not forget.

Baptism

Her grandfather wants to baptize her,
to sprinkle her head with water
in the name of the Father, the Son, and the Holy Ghost.
He is an old man. He
may die.

Her father wants to compromise, to say
Father, Son, Holy Ghost, and
All That Is Divine. It is
his father.

I am the mother.
I know too much of
fathers, sons, and the ghostly things they have done
in the name of the holy.

I want the water on her head
to be rain. I want her watered as our
earth is watered, to live
in the light of the moon:
the crescent, the full, the waning
cycles that pull tides, that pull sea creatures so deep
that sight is only a myth, cycles that pull
bean sprouts through loose soil,
sap up trees, and plush blood from her womb
many moons from now.

I have no need for the supernatural.
Her breath is the miracle. She
is divine.

He wants her blessed in His name.
I want her blessed in her own.

Brown papery leaves

Brown papery leaves rattle in the winter apple orchard.
There is wind today, rare, and sun
and sky smooth heaven-blue.
My baby sleeps in her stroller,
head slumped forward, bobbing now and then
like a person on a bus.

My father died two months ago,
his last car a Mercury.
He decided he didn't need a Cadillac again
and afterwards, was sorry. We were all sorry.
"How many more cars will you buy?" my mother asked.
"Get what you like. We'll still eat the same."
Who could begrudge my father his car?
I use paper on both sides, rinse plastic bags
and my mother saves leftovers, even boiled green beans.
But we all wanted my father to have his car.
He was an immigrant, hungry as a child,
learned to brush his teeth from a well-to-do friend.
He was a sick man. He'd watch the dancers on TV.
"They really can dance," he'd say longingly.

A car passes. My baby wakes, blinks into the sun, smiles,
curls her toes in their knitted booties.
My father loved money, would quote what everything cost,
didn't matter if he was wrong.
He didn't think air pollution, pesticides,
or radiation were very big problems.
He respected doctors, science,
and believed they could cure
whatever we could make.

A big Safeway supermarket was pleasure to him—
the cans lined up with their juicy insides,
the frozen shrimp and sweet pickles,

cinnamon buns, lamb chops.
Driving away he'd say, "That sure was a beautiful store."

If I'd explained it to him. If I'd told him—*Plutonium.*
Dad, plutonium is part of nuclear radiation
and one-millionth of a gram—
that's less than a grain of the sugar you heap in your coffee—
just that is enough
to cause cancer, to damage genes.
It's leaking into our rivers and oceans, potent
for 500,000 years. It's
man-made. Men make it so we have more energy,
so we have garbage disposals, electric can openers,
drive-in banking, master charge, xerox, computers,
bombs, and remote control garage doors.

And Sara, and Jenny and Ben who call you Pop
and pull on you to make puzzles, to draw circles
and circus tents, they will not grow to their old age
because of this. Would it have made any difference?
Would you still have wanted a Cadillac?
Would you still have wanted eight-lane highways
and lights on all night in the Safeway?

Dad, these men are like you. What
can I tell them?
They don't care about whales, buffalo, pelicans.
Birds make no difference to them.
But can they hear *Sara,* Dad?
Sara and *Jenny and Ben?*
Could you?

Swim

You lie under him every
night. In sickness and in health
he has to have you.
You're his warm milk, his night light.

Like a cobra, you writhe
to his flute. He thinks
he's a charmer.

By day you weed the garden,
cook kettles of soup, mock
his feats. You bathe
with your daughter in the lake.

She is nine. Her skin
is brown as a fawn,
her limbs as long, as supple.

You too are brown. You are topaz,
terra umbra. Your limbs
are slender eelgrass.

You swim together
enchanted water snakes
entwining.

Already she fascinates grown men.
They long to
play their flutes to her.

You think you've taught her
how they blunder. By day
she too can weed, can cook,
can swim and laugh at men.

But by night
she's learned what must be done.
She will be captivated, captured.

She will lie under one,
first on starry nights when
his breath is lost in the smell of jasmine
and his mouth is petal soft.

But later, when he has come
from other lovers, when he comes drunk,
when she is ill or pregnant or too soon
after birth or death or
when she has grown to hate him, still
she will lie
under him.

Brown snake, for her
sake, for yours, swim.
Swim away.

The April grasses

flutter, wild
rye, dandelion, wisteria
pale gray-green clusters, lips about to
open, wave their lavender tongues, soften
the air with their sweet breath,
pansies, cornflowers, saffron poppies
broad thin petals thrown back,
and a bush of silver branches thick with tiny
pink blossoms, plumes of pink snow,
and my heart, that fat pink bud,
cowers in its thicket of ribs.

The stranger

An alpha particle emitted by nuclear radiation can damage the regulatory gene of a human cell. After a latency period of five to forty years, the cell will reproduce without limit. We call this cancer.

The stranger fell into her lap, so to speak.
He was spinning, drunk, he
must have been, he fairly flew
into her, bumping others on his way. It was not that
he picked her out, just that his
course landed him there. He fell
into her
lap, he found her soft, she could not help
but let him in. She thought
he was one of her own kind, he
seemed acceptable enough
after the first shock and
a stumble, a fall, one night going too fast—that
could happen to anyone.
And although she bruised
at his arrival, although she noticed something,
a bruise as fruit is sometimes bruised,
she felt fine.

Five summers came, and corn flowers, sweet
william, cock's crown bloomed by the beaches.
The sun went down washing the hills rose, rust, roan,
and the cows cantered the slope for their evening feed,
calves running zig-zags behind.

Ten winters came and rains watered the yellowed fields
until they grew thick velvet green, green clover, chickweed,
sour grass, sorrel.

The sun set early and the cows lay still, their breath
small milky way puffs in the persian blue night
while Taurus, his coal-red eye and cluster of wound stars,
grazed above.

Fifteen springs came. Children ran barefoot among the ferns
along the soggy river bank, jumping rocks, feeling the current
swirl their feet. Camellias bloomed like roses, apple
and lemon trees fluttered pink and white petals and
acacias billowed, bellowed their yellow release.

Twenty autumns came. Cows rasped the salt block and chomped
tops of prickly pear; the people pressed apples to thick cider;
pumpkins, squash, carrots, maple leaves, all turned orange as the
harvest moon.
The ocean, in grays and blues, greens and sunset flamingo,
then smoke, then black, cresting white,
the ocean rolled in over herself, rolling over herself, over herself,
over and over.

And the woman, planting marigolds, planting white corn,
carrying her babies, watching them crumble
long stemmed leaves
in their curious fists, washing her hair, writing letters,
buying coffee in town,
the woman no longer thought about the stranger.

If you had asked her, reminded her, perhaps she would have
remembered, laughed, *oh yes*.
But twenty years is a long time and she probably forgot.
Certainly when she noticed
she did not think of him.

She had born children before: the rise,
the swelling; as the pulsing begins, the

gripping in her womb, the hardening and
softening, and faster until this being
plops from her being and the one become two.
She had born many children. Her house
was filled with children. And they, in their
season, had born children. Like the cows
and the horses, the mollusks, the corn flowers,
camellias, and gulls. One
becomes two, becomes four, becomes more.
In its season, in plenty. There was always plenty.
So she did not notice at first, when
one slept on the sofa and the butter did not last the week.
She did not notice when several slept on the living room floor
and they ran out of beans and hot water. She paid little
mind when they pitched tents in the back yard and
there were no eggs for breakfast and the wood pile was gone.
There were plenty of hands to chop more. And she wasn't really
worried though they no longer could sit down to dinner and she was missing
all her socks and hadn't seen her oldest daughter for some time now.
And when the flour bin was empty and the septic tank full and
no one had chopped more wood and the cold water was a trickle
and the children in her bed were hungry strangers yanking on an empty rubber
nipple, she worried then.
But by then it was too late.

They were grabbing at the last vegetables in the garden,
the turnips, the potatoes, pushing
each other aside, the big ones were
nasty by now, the saliva
rolled in their mouths. They ate
the roots. They ate the snails, the flies, the grubs.
They ate the milk cows, the dogs and the cats.
They ate the newspapers, the paint off the sills, the silk curtains, the
dust curls.
They ate each other's feces and their own. And slowly,
eventually, they all died.

For Saraswati, at eight months

She grasped my finger
when she nursed as an infant,
grounding herself in the firm connection.
Now her fingers scuttle lightly
over mine. I stroke her wrist
with one fingertip, she strokes
my thumb. We skim each other
like night breezes, dancers
in a *pas de deux*.
Our hands are willow branches in full leaf,
we rustle. We twine
like cypress roots reflected in the river, we
shimmer.

Years ago I slept with a lover
in a small blue carpeted room.
At night my hands found each other, arms rising
like funnels of smoke, like silk scarves,
fingertips grazing their length like honey bees.

Mornings, he told me, "Your hands
they have a life of their own. I'm afraid
what they might do." In time
I learned to sleep like others, arms
abandoned heavily on the bed.

With her
I know the night again. She calls me
in the cool dark, her fingers rove
over my palm, warm rain on the shallow basin,
across my knuckles, the flat back of my hand,
the mound of my thumb. My fingers tremble
on her skin. Loons
skimming the lake, water
trembling.

Leave-taking

for Paula

Oranges sit in a wooden bowl,
small cauterized circles where the stems were broken.
When I tear the rind
the bitter oil sprays fine like breast milk,
but pungent.
Paula gave me the oranges.
Paula is leaving.

I held back, did not
seek you out, did not offer tea
when you brought pears
from your tree, each green fruit
dried in a towel.

And when you drove me to the doctor
while my belly grew,
weeks so hot our blouses clung to our backs,
and told me I needn't use baby powder, vaseline,
or keep water in the diaper pail, I
simply thanked you.

When Sara was born and you sent tulips,
brought squeaky moo cows and silver shells for me,
I was glad to see you, but I was not tender.

You talked too much, I thought. You
moved too fast. You cooked hamburger and minute rice.
You might
want something back.

But you were the one who took my child when I had to buy groceries
and my mother'd gone home
and Alan left for work saying, "How do other women manage?"

You were the one I called when his father was sick,
when my father died.
You cancelled my classes, took my place at readings,
fed the dog.

I called you when Sara had a cold.
I called every night.
"She won't nurse. She can't breathe."
You read me Dr. Spock
and half the Encyclopedia of Children's Medicine.

You were the one who showed me she could gum a crust of bread.
"She's eating it!" I marvelled.
"Everybody likes french bread," you said.

It was in your house she first drank from a cup.
You sloshed it over her chin and shirt
while she gulped big fish gulps.
"Hers is greedy," you sang.

Every Thursday when you picked her up
your youngest called, "Sawa! Sawa!" from the car,
and when I arrived, you'd be reading a book,
having knit a sweater big enough for both of us,
made dinner, driven to and from soccer practice
and written two chapters of your novel, while Sara
crawled calmly among the four small boys playing football on the lawn.

I didn't mean to, but (not even I
could turn away such gifts) I've grown
to love you, I love you,
the inflections of your voice, your heavy hair
held back with red barrettes, your small hand,

the way you reached your hand to me—
you were driving, I was crying—you reached
and covered my hand.

Paula, you led me through this passage
for which there was no ritual.
No mothers with strong browned hands rubbed my breasts with oil
or twined olive leaves into my hair.
No elders chanted a dirge for the woman who was dying
or blessed with the patience of date groves, the mother being born.
There was no incense, no offering of grain, no moonlight, no dawn.
Only phone calls from electric kitchens,
me standing amidst books, pots, dripping juice bottles
and you, on the other end, in your own pile of blocks and cracker crumbs,
talking me through.

There will never be another year like this, this
first birth happens only once. My need
will never be that need again.
You have been my mother
as I became a mother.

It is early summer. You leave tomorrow.
We sit on your porch. Pears hang, tight pendants
from your trees. We will never sit here again.

Your children are making tents with blankets and chairs
in the living room, Sara has fallen asleep on the bed.
For these few moments, we are alone. You say,
"You are beautiful." I say, "I will never forget you."
Only bees stir the jasmine scented air.

Then your husband comes through the sliding doors
with briefcase and Sara crying in his arms, the
children insisting, "We didn't wake her, honest Mom."
I leave quickly.

Driving home, the setting sun tightening my eyelids
I see your face.

Let every woman

We are going to be given equality,
they tell us. Soon
they will draft us
along with the men.

But there is nothing new
in women working for the army.

We have carried, birthed, and suckled sons,
heaped mashed potatoes onto their plates,
fried thousands of hamburgers. Some of us
have grown the potatoes, some have fed the cows,
all have washed the dishes afterward.

We have driven our sons to little league
and paid for the corsages of baby roses
they pinned on dates for proms.

We have worn corsages to proms.
We have kissed good-bye at bus stations
and promised sweethearts to be true.

We have waved good-bye from train platforms,
we have waved good-bye from the windows of airports,
we have kissed and waved good-bye to sons, lovers, fathers—
        our own, and the fathers of our children.

We have knit socks and rolled bandages.
We have traveled with the troops,
nursing, typing, performing in sequinned gowns, entwining
our bodies in the night, raising children.

We have entered the workforce.
We have withdrawn from the workforce.
We have tingled at the sight of a man in uniform.

We have sent tins of sardines, chocolate chip cookies,
smiling photographs, and newsy, perfumed letters.

And some of us have received letters,
on embossed stationery, "Dear Madam."

Some of us have received boxes.

Some of the boxes could not be opened.

Our sons have killed the sons of British women,
the sons of British women have killed the sons of German women,
the sons of German women have killed our sons.

> How many mothers
> have received their dead?
> How many dream he is alive
> wake in the night, night after night?

Our sons, our husbands, our lovers have raped the daughters of
Mexican women, of Japanese women, of Cambodian women,
and their sons, husbands, and lovers have raped others.

> How many women have been raped?
> Raped at gun-point, knife-point,
> tied with ropes, gang-raped,
> raped with rifles, raped with bayonets?
> How many have been raped beside their children, children
> raped beside their mothers?

Our fathers gave blankets infected with smallpox to Native Americans.
Our brothers napalmed Viet Nam, dropped agent orange on rice paddies.

Our children and the children of the Viet Namese women
are born malformed.

> How many children gasp for breath?
> How many retarded? How many anesthetized
> as surgeons saw their skulls,
> bone won't grow, brain pressing?
> How many are born without stomach,
> without skin? How many
> stillborn?

Now, nuclear weapons—
this country can drop bombs on that country.
But wind and rain do not obey a general's orders.
As we kill them, we kill ourselves,
we kill our own children, we sentence our children's children.

> Women mourning, sitting shivah, keening at wakes,
> dressing in black, tearing their dresses,
> wailing, ululating, voices piercing the toll of bells,
> women screaming, women moaning, women
> wiping their tears with handkerchiefs, with hands,
> not bothering.
> Women dry-eyed setting breakfast before the rest
> of their families.
> Women sitting up through the night, maybe sewing.

We grieve, we pay taxes, we give to the Red Cross.
We worked for the army before we got the vote
and after we got the vote,
before we were admitted to schools
and after we were admitted to schools,
before we were drafted—

there is nothing new
in women working for the army.

Let every woman who loves a woman resist,
every woman who remembers her mother, her mother's hand
        gentle on her brow   in fever
        cold wet washcloths, sips of 7-up,
who remembers her grandmother, her grandmother's hands
        loose mottled flesh, holding hers as they jump the waves, singing
        by the sea, by the sea, resist.

Resist. Let every woman who loves a man resist.
her father pulling her on the sled,
        the smell of wet wool, mittens, her warm breath in the muffler.

Let every woman who remembers her first love resist,
        how the leaves blushed that autumn
        and the black silhouettes of trees against the winter twilight
        raised an ache so sweet
        she did not want to go inside, not ever

Resist. Let every woman resist,
every woman who has opened her bones, pushed out new life,
        who has suckled a baby in the silent night.

Let every woman who loves a cat resist,
a hawk, a tulip—
                        nothing is spared—
                                                resist.

Let every woman who has been raped, resist,
abused, resist,
beaten, resist,
who has feared, resist.

Who has met her fury,
who has seen her face reflected in the moon,
let every woman who loves herself, resist,

who has eaten blackberries warm off the bush,
who has felt water pouring into her palm,
who has witnessed the seedling raise green arms into the sun drenched air,

resist.

Gertrude Käsebier

> ". . . on a European trip, she discovered her true vocation as a photographer. Without the customary conveniences of darkroom work, she would wait until . . . night . . . to carry wet plates down to a river to be washed."
>
> —from *In Her Own Image: Women Working in the Arts*
> ed. Elaine Hedges and Ingrid Wendt

The water over slick plates, river water
dark, thick, warm
as water is at night.

She pushes back her skirt, her sleeves
rolled above the elbow, dips her hands into the water,
soft, heavy, flooding the plates.

They told her *photography is not creative.*
She believed them
until now, these nights

her fingertips grooved like the sand of river beds,
the willow and black alder rustling, the owl's *hoo hoo*
resonating, she can feel its tremor in the water.
Wet. The wet scent of river mud, river grass.

Water is the color of night, liquid
black without reflection. River stones, the soft turf
of river bank, her own arms and hands
are vague in the shallow star light.

All night she crouches,
her knees imprinted with wet folds of her skirts,
her hands certain, familiar to water, fish.

All night the images emerge
in imperceptible degrees, as she dips and rinses,
dips and rinses, the rush of river
obscuring that faint hum of planets

until the lightening of
mass into form, shadow,
shades of gray, pale
tinge of color, dawn.
She gathers up her plates.

Walking back to the house she shivers,
thinks about breakfast, ham, buttered toast
in a pewter rack, the next night.

After birth

The glint of it, in the low autumn sun,
shining, trailing from her, sea-red ragged train.

She, the cow, turning, stepping, her head
reaching for it, circling, while the calf lies
damp, matted. She circles, circles, then
giving it up, licks the calf's head, ears, neck,
her nose under its breast, under its foreleg,
licking upward, butting, raising the calf to stand
legs splayed, its own thin umbilicus hanging pale.

The calf hobbles, knees, ankles buckling.
It nuzzles her side, her breast, its head butting up
with the same jerk the older calves make
as they grab and pull the thick milk.

I look down at my own child, biting her apple,
small nips she crushes between teeth that have
pushed up like coral out of the sea.
She sucks her mouthful of apple bits, mashing them dry,
then spews them out. They lie like red and white
confetti about her. When I turn back

the calf has found the teat, the afterbirth has
fallen, lies, a shallow lake, on the green and brown grass.
The calf sucks, the cow licks the placenta,
lifting it into her grinding teeth, chewing,
chewing as it hangs from her jaw,
dark, tough.

Tell me the stories, Mama

You are going into surgery. You are
across the continent
in a blue and white kitchen
on the eleventh floor of a condominium
overlooking the ocean. Right now
as I finish a late lunch, you are making
your dinner, perhaps chicken.

I have the surgeon's name and number.
I will ask him questions
from pencilled notes. Patiently
he will explain by-pass, dye-test,
pressure cuff, degree of closure.
I will thank him too profusely,
hang up, feeling my questions
unanswered. You

are the one I want to ask, you
know the stories, tell me again
how your mother sent you to the store
for onions when you were a little girl. A nickel or perhaps three cents
for a bag of onions. Tell me how she said you can always put in an extra
onion. Onions are cheap. When you got to the store you saw licorice,
sour balls, chocolate kisses. You bought a pocketful.
"What did she say?" I'd ask you. "What did she say?"
"What could she say?" you'd tell me. "It was done."

I need to hear again
when Grandmom married, the women in her cigar factory all chipped in
a dollar and bought her a crystal cut-glass bowl. Eighteen women.
Eighteen dollars. It was a small fortune and shone in the light.
Long after your father left she took pleasure from the bowl.
But there were five children, the apartment was small, and one day,
it had to happen: Jack knocked Norman or Norman knocked Jack and the bowl
shattered. When Grandmom came back from the store she didn't say anything.

The tears just began to flow. She cried all the rest of the day,
making dinner, putting the younger children to bed, silent, the tears
slipping down her cheeks.

Remind me
how in nurses' training, when the girls went to the movies,
they all returned red-eyed but you. The supervisor asked, "Miss Wolpert,
how is it you're not crying?" "I've seen too much in life," you said.

Tell me how you met Dad, he was your patient.
His eyes were bandaged, but he said he could tell you
were coming by the sound of your footsteps.

I want to remember the name of the street where you first lived.
I know you didn't cook. Meals were free at the hospital
and Dad ate at his mother's. But sometimes you'd look around the kitchen,
worried if your father came to visit, you'd have nothing to serve.
He never came. You'd bake, in case.

Tell me about the move to Fresno, how you went for the climate
hoping it would help Dad's health. There were no houses,
you lived in a hotel room. Herb's teacher called you into school.
He was wearing short pants and high socks like boys did in the east.
She said, "The other children make fun of him, buy him long pants."

Tell me how Dad hurt his knee, he was kneeling making a display
at J.C. Penney's, I can't remember—wallets or ties—what the display was,
tell me

how long he was in the hospital, how you'd walk Herb to school
then walk to the hospital, 3,000 miles from home, from family, and
you'd tell me, even though your heart was breaking, the sun
would be shining down on you, the air filled with lemon blossoms,
still you'd feel grateful to be alive.

Tell me the stories, Mama. I need to hear you talk.
Pour a highball, set it on a yellow paper napkin.
I want to hear them again and again
until I can tell them like you.

Language

There is no word
for a woman giving birth,
for a first birth,
for a new mother.
Eskimos have forty-seven
words for snow.

There are times in life when one does the right thing

the thing one will not regret,
when the child wakes crying "mama", late
as you are about to close your book and sleep
and she will not be comforted back to her crib,
she points you out of her room, into yours,
you tell her, "I was just reading here in bed,"
she says, "read a book," you explain it's not a children's book
but you sit with her anyway, she lays her head on your breast,
one-handed, you hold your small book, silently read,
resting it on the bed to turn pages
and she, thumb in mouth, closes her eyes, drifts,
not asleep—when you look down at her, her lids open,
and once you try to carry her back
but she cries, so you return to your bed again and book,
and the way a warmer air will replace a cooler with a slight
shift of wind, or swimming, entering a mild current, you
enter this pleasure, the quiet book, your daughter in your lap,
an articulate person now, able to converse, yet still
her cry is for you, her comfort in you,
it is your breast she lays her head upon,
you are lovers, asking nothing but this bodily presence.
She hovers between sleep, you read your book,
you give yourself this hour, sweet and quiet beyond flowers
beyond lilies of the valley and lilacs even, the smell of her breath,
the warm damp between her head and your breast. Past midnight
she blinks her eyes, wiggles toward a familiar position,
utters one word, "sleeping." You carry her swiftly into her crib,
cover her, close the door halfway, and it is this sense of rightness,
that something has been healed, something
you will never know, will never have to know.

OUR STUNNING HARVEST

Our Stunning Harvest

I.

She recognizes miner's lettuce
nibbles its round leaf.
Her father asks *Do you know*
not to eat the other plants?
and she nods solemnly.
We have taught her not to swallow pits
of cherries or olives.
She spits them out bald
and repeats *Could make a child sick.*
And walking, when we hear a car
she runs to the side of the road
stands, stationary, until it passes.
But how do I protect her
from men who rape children?
from poison in the air?
from nuclear holocaust?

I walk this road—oak trees, eucalyptus
blackberry bushes in white flower
the hard green fruit pushing out behind the blossoms—
the first time I have walked here alone
since that day almost two years ago
when I carried her in my belly,
the morning before her birth.
It was dustier then, drought
the smell of hot clay and stillness
in the tall Queen Anne's lace.
Today the breeze is cool.
But the dread, the urgency
etch my pleasure like acid.

I clean house, shove socks and shirts
in the washer, speed through the grocery,

type, fold, staple—
but what good are dishes stacked in the cupboard,
peaches and avocadoes in the basket, envelopes
stamped in the dark mailbox?

At night I lie in bed imagining what I will do if attacked—
alone, I could run
or fight
but with her—in the stroller, holding my hand
on this country road?
A mother bird flutters and distracts.
She risks her life, but the babies are protected.
I could not even protect her.
She is too small to run. If I whispered *run*
should would not go. And if I tried to carry her
we would be overcome. I could not fight with her
not far from help. I am prey.
With her as hostage
I am blackmailed.
And if I am not enough? if they want her too?

My husband sleeps by my side
his regular sleep breath. I
lean closer, try to absorb
the calm. But the possibilities do not stop.
I don't let them. I keep trying scenarios,
get as far as convincing the rapist to let me take her to a neighbor
then rushing into the house, locking him out.
But he may not even speak English
I sober myself, and besides . . .

I am sick in the night, sick the next day.
My stomach won't digest food, it runs through me
foul, waste.
By noon I fall asleep, she sleeps in the crook of my arm.
We sleep for hours. For these few hours
we are safe.
I know we have been safe
afterward.

II.

Yesterday I read they tried to kill Dr. Rosalie Bertell,
a nun who researched radiation-caused cancer. Here,
the resource center for non-violence is shot up,
tires slashed.

My husband is limiting his practice
so he can work against nuclear destruction.
He says *We may be in danger, you know.*
If the steering on the car ever feels funny
pull right over.
He's had the lug nuts loosened before.

But we both know that is not the greatest danger.
Radiation from Love Creek, Churchrock, Rocky Flats,
Three Mile Island, West Valley, Hanford–
we live near the San Andreas Fault–
an earthquake
and the Diablo Canyon plant
could kill millions–
and bombs, Trident, the draft beginning again.
Who are these madmen
whose lives are so barren, so desperate
they love nothing?

What will it take to make them change?
What will it take?

What will it take to make *me* change?
I still use plastic bags from Dow Chemical.
When am I
going to stop?

I ask my friend. She smiles.
Polyvinylchloride poisons your food she says.

What do you do with your lettuce? I ask.

Glass jars, or a pot with a lid.

I smile.
I have a pot with a lid.

What good will one woman never again using plastic bags do
in the face of tons of plutonium, recombinant DNA
a hundred thousand rapists?
What good does it do that I feed my daughter organic rice
purple beets, never sugar?
What good that I march with other women
and we yell *WOMEN UNITED*
WILL NEVER BE DEFEATED
banshees into the night?

These things will not save my daughter.
I know. I know that.
But unless I do them
she will not be saved

and I want to save her.
Oh Mother of us all, I am a mother too
I want to save her.

III.

I want to talk to the president.
I want to go with other mothers
and meet with the president.
And I want mothers from Russia there.
And the head of Russia.
And Chinese mothers
and the head of China
and mothers from Saudi Arabia and Japan and South Africa
and all the heads of state and the families of the heads of state
and the children, all the children of the mothers.
I want a meeting.

I want to ask the president, *Is there nothing
precious to you?*

And when the president explains how it's the
Russians, I want the Russian women to say *We don't
want war*. I want all the women to scream *We don't want war, we,
the people, do not want war.*

And I want the president to admit he wants war,
he wants power and money and war more
than he wants the lives of his children.
I want to see him turn to his children and tell them
they will not live, that
no one will live,
that with one computer error all life on this planet can be
annihilated, that two men could go mad and push one button
in a silo, in a plane, that these men do go mad,
the men with access to the buttons go mad all the time,
are replaced, that one
might not be replaced soon enough.

I want each head of state to tell his children what will happen
if any country sends a thermonuclear bomb,
I want each head of state, with his own tongue, to tell his children
how the computers of the other country would pick up the signal,
how they would fire back, how the bombs would hit.
I want each president and prime minister and king
to tell his children how firestorms would burn, vaporizing people,
animals, plants, and then as days passed,
how the millions would die of radiation sickness,
their skin sloughing off, the nausea, hair falling out,
hemorrhage, infection, no hospitals, no clean water,
the stench of dead and decaying bodies, bacteria and virus rampant,
insects rampant, and the radiation ticking, ticking
as millions more die over the next years, leukemia, cancer, and no hope
for the future, birth deformity, stillbirth, miscarriage, sterility,
millions and billions.

I want them to watch the faces of their children.
I want them to watch their eyes pale
the flecks of light fading,
and when their children ask *Why?*
I want them to point to the other heads of state
and the others to point back
and I want the mothers screaming.
I want the mothers of the children of the heads of state screaming.
I want them to scream until their voices are hoarse whispers
raw as the bloody rising of the sun, I want them to hiss

How dare you?
How dare you?
Kill them yourself, then.
Kill them here, now, with your own hands.

Kill all these children, clench
your hands around their necks, crunch their spines.
Kill one
two, three, kill hundreds. If you are going to kill
then kill.

I want to see the faces of the president, the premier, the prime minister,
the chancellor, the king.
I want to see their faces tremble.
I want to see them tremble like a still lake under wind.
I want to see them weep.

I must be crazy myself.
My mother is an optimist. She believes in a survival instinct.
She has read the statistics, knows
plutonium is poison for 500,000 years.
But she does not think of these things.
It depresses her, she says.

I say she is naive.
But I write poems in which presidents and premiers weep
at the voices of raging mothers. I write
they weep.
I must be crazy. I am crazy.
And I want this meeting like a crazy woman wants.

I want to go myself.
I want my daughter to ride her four-wheeled horse around the carpeted room,
fast, steering with her red sneakered feet through
potted plants and filing cabinets,
precise, dauntless.

I want her spirit to inspire us.
I don't want to hear about numbers.
I don't want to hear one number about how many bombs or how much money
or dates or megatons or anything else.
I want to hear *No more.*
I want to hear *My child will not be murdered.*
My child will live.

I want to dance victorious, to dance and dance
ring around the rosie, with no one falling down.
No ashes, no ashes.
I want no ashes from my child's tender head.
I want to dance. I want to sing. I want to kiss all the heads of state,
all the mothers, every child.
I want to kiss them all and dance the hora, dance the mazurka,
the waltz, the tribal dances, bare feet on red clay
on white sand
on black earth
dancing, kissing, singing
dancing, dancing until our legs are strong
our arms strong, our thighs, lungs, bellies strong,
until our voices are loud, clear, and vibrate with the wind
until we ride the wind
until we ride home, with the wind, flying, flying
laughing, kissing, singing, cackling, our children
tucked under our wings, safe.
Safe. We are safe. We are so strong.
We can protect our children.

IV.

No you won't, the young, composed woman taunts us
slowly, from the stage.
She is our teacher. She is teaching us our power.

Yes we will, we yell back.

No you won't.

Yes we will.

No you won't.

We are roaring, *YES WE WILL. YES WE WILL.*

Now she pauses *Say*, *Yes* I *Will.*

Yes I will, I yell.

AGAIN, she bellows.

Yes I will, my eyes fill with tears. I am trembling.
YES I WILL. YES I WILL. YES I WILL.

I will.
I will protect my daughter.
How
will I protect my daughter?

Even if we dismantle the bombs, cement the power plants,
ban 2,4,5-T, men are still raping women.

Men raped women before they split the atom
before they concocted herbicides in their stainless steel laboratories.
They raped in war and they raped in what they called peace,
they raped in marriage,

they raped in groups, they raped old women, young women,
they raped when they were angry, they raped when they were scorned,
they raped when they got drunk, got high, got a weekend pass,
got on the Dean's list, got fired. They still do.

They rape women asleep, children asleep—
                    fathers have easy access to children asleep.
They rape babies—
                    doctors treat thre-month-old babies for gonorrhea
                    of the throat.

They rape women getting into their cars after late night shifts,
they rape old women washing up their breakfast dishes,
they call on the phone and threaten rape, they write songs like
your lips tell me no no, but there's yes yes in your eyes,
they design high heeled sandals so we can't run away,
they invent the pill—easy sex and we die from cancer when they're done.

They use knives and guns when subtler coercion is not enough,
sometimes they use the knives and guns anyway, afterward.

And how shall I protect her?
How shall we protect each other?

I can warn her not to talk to strangers
I can forbid her to go out at night

I can nag her to press her knees together
        and buttton her blouses to her neck,
but none of that will assure her safety
or even her survival.

I can enroll her in self-defense, judo, karate.
I can practice with her in our yard. We can grow
quick and deft, together.
And that will help, but it is not enough.
Three boys with razor blades, a man with a .45 . . .

We can castrate rapists. My mother suggested that.
She thinks simply, and I like the idea.
But the damage is already done, and the next time
they can use a broken bottle, it's not sex they want.
So what's enough? what's enough?

Only
to gather,
to gather as our foremothers gathered.
Wild plants, berries, nuts—they were gatherers
they gathered together, their food, their sustenance
reeds for weaving baskets, feathers, raven and flamingo
dyes, ochre and vermilion,
they gathered flat stones for pounding
scooped stones for grinding, they gathered rocks, they gathered
shells and the meat of the shells—conch, mussel, clam, they
gathered wood for fire, they gathered clay from the riverbank
they kneaded the clay, they pinched and pressed it with their fingers
they shaped bowls and jars, they baked the vessels

in the coals of the fire, they gathered water, they gathered rain
they gathered honey, they gathered the stories of their mothers
their grandmothers, they gathered under moonlight
they danced, the feel of cool packed dirt under feet
they sang praises, they cried prayers.
When attacked, they knew how to gather their fingers into a fist
they could jab with sharpened sticks, they could hurl rock.
They gathered their strength, they gathered together
they gathered the blessings of the goddess, their faith
in the turning of the earth, the seasons bleeding into each other
                    leaves crumbled into earth, earth
                    sprouting water-green leaves
they gathered leaves, chickweed, comfrey, plantain, nettles
they worked together, they fought together
they fed, they bathed, they suckled their young,
they gathered stars into constellations
and their reflections into shallow bowls of water,
they gathered an acknowledged, familiar harmony
one I have never known, one I long for
long to gather
with all you women.

V.

Women, I want
to gather with you.
Our numbers are grand.
Our hands are capable, practised,
our minds know pattern, know
relationship, how the tree
pulls water up through root
through trunk, through branch, stem
into leaf, how the surface stomata release
water vapor into the air, the air cooled. We know
to honor trees. We know
the chrysalis, the grub, the earthworm.
We have handled baby poop and vomit
the incontinence of the old and sick.
We smell menses every month
from the time we are young girls.
We do not faint.
We do not titter
at mice.
We have handled horses, tractors
scalpels, saws.
We have handled money
and the lack of it
and we have survived

poverty, puerperal fever
forceps, scopolamine
footbinding, excision, infibulation
beatings, thorazine, diet pills
rape, witch burning, valium, chin lifts
female infanticide, child molestation
breast x-rays, suttee.

Some of us have died. Millions, millions
have been killed, murdered. We
mourn, we mourn
their courage, their innocence
their wisdom often lost to us.
We remember.
We are fierce
like a cornered animal.
Our fury spurts like geysers
like volcanoes, brilliant lava, molten gold
cascading in opulent plumes.

And every morning we gather eggs from the chickens
we milk the goat
or drive to the Safeway and push our cart
under fluorescent lights
We feed our children.

We feed them blood from our womb
milk at our breast.
Our bodies create and nourish life.

We create. Alone
we are able to create.
Parthenogenesis. Two eggs unite. It happens.
It has always happened.
One woman, alone, can create life.
Think what all of us could do

if we gather
gather like the ocean gathers for the wave

the cloud gathers for the storm
the uterus gathers for contraction
the pushing out, the birth.

We can gather.
We can save our earth.
We can labor like we labored
to birth our babies,
laboring past thirst, past the rising and the setting of the sun
past distraction, past demands
past the need to pee, to cry, or even to live
into the consuming pain
pain
pain beyond possibility,
until there is nothing but the
inevitable gathering
gathering, gathering
and

the new is born
relief spreading through us
like the wave after cresting
spreads over sand in a shush of foam, grace
our saving grace.

VI.

NO touch bee
BITE my finger
my daughter explains to me
pulling back her hand from the wild radish blossoms
    buzzing with furry bees.

My child
with your neck still creased in slight folds
the tiny white hairs of your back stemming up your spine
fanning out over shoulders like a fern,
you *may* live
you *may*, you *may*, oh I want to believe it is possible
the you may live
to handle bees, pick miner's lettuce
eat black olives in the sun,
  to gather,
    with me
      with your daughters
        with all the world's life-sweet women,
          our stunning harvest.

About the Author

ELLEN BASS has won the Elliston Book Award for Poetry and is co-editor of *No More Masks! An Anthology of Poems by Women* (Doubleday) and *I Never Told Anyone: Writings by Women Survivors of Child Sexual Abuse* (Harper & Row). Her poem "Our Stunning Harvest", which appeared in *Reweaving the Web of Life: Feminism and Nonviolence* (New Society Publishers), has been read and performed across the country by antinuclear activists. Travelling nationally, Ellen leads "I Never Told Anyone" workshops for survivors and "Writing About Our Lives" workshops for all women, As a lesbian and a feminist, Ellen is realizing her vision of gathering with women to heal, to create, and to celebrate.

More Resources From New Society Publishers

To Order: send check or money order to New Society Publishers, 4722 Baltimore Avenue, Philadelphia, PA 19143. For postage and handling: add $1.50 for the first book and 40 cents for each additional book.

WE ARE ALL PART OF ONE ANOTHER: A BARBARA DEMING READER
edited with an introduction by Jane Meyerding
Foreword by Barbara Smith

Essays, speeches, letters, stories, poems by America's foremost writer on issues of women and peace, feminism and nonviolence, spanning four decades.

"Barbara Deming always challenges us to rise above easy answers about who we are. Her insight into the nature of political change and the needs of the human spirit makes hers a unique feminist voice which guides and inspires us in the struggle for a more humane world."
—Charlotte Bunch

320 pages. 1984.
Hardcover: $24.95
Paperback: $10.95

REWEAVING THE WEB OF LIFE: FEMINISM AND NONVIOLENCE
edited by Pam McAllister

". . . happens to be one of the most important books you'll ever read."
—*The Village Voice*

"Stressing the connection between patriarchy and war, sex and violence, this book shows that nonviolence can be an assertive, positive force. It's provocative reading for anyone interested in surviving and changing the nuclear age."
—*Ms. Magazine*

More than 50 contributors. Topics include: Women's History, Women and the Struggle Against Militarism, Violence and its Origins, Nonviolence and Women's Self-Defense. A richly varied collection of interviews, songs, poems, stories, provocative proposals, photographs.

Most often recommended book in the 1983 WIN MAGAZINE ANNUAL BOOK POLL

Annotated Bibliography. Index.
448 pages.
Hardcover: $19.95
Paperback: $10.95

OUR FUTURE AT STAKE: A TEEN-AGERS GUIDE TO STOPPING THE NUCLEAR ARMS RACE

by Melinda Moore & Laurie Olsen, Citizens Policy Center

"The problem with getting my friends involved with the nuclear issue is that they don't know enough about it or even where to get information. I am their teacher now. I give them plenty of information whether they like it or not."

—Lena Flores, 17

Informative, beautifully illustrated and photographed resource for education and action. Includes personal statements by teenagers themselves. Handy glossary and chronology for teenagers seeking to understand the nuclear arms madness. Ideal for school, church and community groups.

Illustrated. 68 pages. Large format. 1984.
Hardcover: $19.95
Paperback: $6.95

RESOURCE MANUAL FOR A LIVING REVOLUTION

by Virginia Coover, Ellen Deacon, Charles Esser and Christopher Moore

The practical tools you need for everything from consciousness raising, working in groups, and developing communities of support to education, training, and organizing skills. Used by women's groups, disarmament and antinuclear activists, and community organizers worldwide. 25,000 copies in print. An activist's dream!

330 pages. Agendas. Exercises.
Hardcover: $19.95
Paperback: $9.95

GANDHI THROUGH WESTERN EYES

by Horace Alexander

"This book stands out as an authoritative guide: clear, simple, and straightforward, both to Gandhi's personality and to his beliefs. As a Quaker, Mr. Alexander could easily grasp Gandhi's ideas about nonviolence; the author's prolonged and intimate friendship helped him to know the Mahatma as few men were able to do, and to appreciate that he was something far greater than a national hero of the Indian independence movement—a man, in fact, with a message that is intensely relevant for the world today. Nothing that has so far been published about Gandhi is more illuminating than this careful, perceptive and comprehensive work. It is not only comprehensive—it is convincing." —*Times Literary Supplement*

Letter, Index. 240 pages. 1984.
Hardcover: $24.95
Paperback: $8.95

A MANUAL ON NONVIOLENCE AND CHILDREN

compiled and edited by Stephanie Judson; Foreword by Paula J. Paul, Educators for Social Responsibility

Includes "For the Fun of It! Selected Cooperative Games for Children and Adults"

Invaluable resource for creating an atmosphere in which children and adults can resolve problems and conflicts nonviolently. Especially useful for parents and teachers in instilling values today to create the peacemakers of tomorrow!

"Stephanie Judson's excellent manual has helped many parents and teachers with whom we have worked. An essential part of learning nonviolent ways of resolving conflicts is the creation of a trusting, affirming and cooperative environment in the home and classroom. This manual has a wealth of suggestions for creating such an environment. We highly recommend it."

—Jim and Kathy McGinnis,
Parenting for Peace and Justice, St. Louis, Missouri

Illustrated, large format. 160 pages. 1984.
Hardcover: $24.95
Paperback: $9.95

MORE THAN THE TROUBLES: A COMMON SENSE VIEW OF THE NORTHERN IRELAND CONFLICT

by Lynne Shivers & David Bowman, SJ

"Religion is only one factor among the many differing traditions, cultural and historical allegiances that separate the people of Northern Ireland, according to this thoughtful, excellent reference book. Shivers, a Quaker activist and writer, and Bowman, a director of the Jesuit International Ecumenical Committee and a consultant on Ireland to the National Council of Churches, trace the historical origins and present exacerbations of major issues that fuel the struggle. The authors, adherents of nonviolence and active sponsors of peacemaking groups, present an objective and detailed explanation of the two basic ideologies that polarize Northern Ireland, and the dozens of political parties, quasi-political organizations, security forces and paramilitary groups that represent them."

—*Publishers Weekly*

240 pages. Index. Appendices. Maps. Charts.
Bibliography. Photographs. 1984.
Hardcover: $24.95

HANDBOOK FOR SATYAGRAHIS: A MANUAL FOR VOLUNTEERS OF TOTAL REVOLUTION

by Narayan Desai

India's foremost trainer in nonviolent action presents an integrated, practical approach to training for radical social change, growing out of the experience of the Gandhian movement.
57 pages. $3.95

A SEX REVOLUTION
by Lois Waisbrooker

With an introduction "Women in the Lead: Waisbrooker's Way to Peace" by Pam McAllister, editor of *Reweaving the Web of Life: Feminism and Nonviolence.*

In her own day, Lois Waisbrooker was called "the Abraham Lincoln of women". A dynamic speaker and writer, anarchist, spiritualist, and feminist, she advocated "women's control over their own bodies".

In her novel *A Sex Revolution*, women demand control of the world for fifty years to see whether it leads to the abolition of war. The book is a strikingly contemporary condemnation of the masculine concept of "defense by the State" which has placed us on the brink of nuclear annihilation.

160 pages. 1985.
Hardcover: $19.95
Paperback: $6.95

LEADERSHIP FOR CHANGE: TOWARD A FEMINIST MODEL
by Bruce Kokopeli and George Lakey

Reject authoritarian and paternalistic forms of leadership. Making practical use of feminist perspectives, break leadership functions down into their component parts to be shared and rotated, empowering all.

32 pages. Illustrated. $2.45

OFF THEIR BACKS. . .AND ON OUR OWN TWO FEET
by Men Against Patriarchy

This pamphlet addressed to men includes three essays: "More Power Than We Want: Masculine Sexuality and Violence," "Understanding, and Fighting Sexism," and "Overcoming Masculine Oppression in Mixed Groups."

32 pages. 1983. $2.45

WOMEN IN DEVELOPMENT: A RESOURCE GUIDE FOR ORGANIZATION AND ACTION

by ISIS Women's International Information and Communication Service.

A lavishly illustrated book, with 122 photographs, five years in the making. Women scholars from all over the world contributed to make this one of the most comprehensive and beautiful books of its kind ever published. Sections on women and multinationals, women and rural development, women and health, education, tourism, migration, etc.

Annotated resource lists, bibliographies. 240 pages. 1984.
Hardcover: $39.95
Paperback: $14.95

THE EYE OF THE CHILD

by Ruth Mueller

A brilliant healing myth for a world gone mad!

"Of all the creatures to whom the great mother had given birth all were a part, not apart, but one. Yes all but one flowed as she flowed, born of her womb, dying in her bosom, struggling, true, but never against their own life support. One, only one, capable of standing apart, imagining self above and outside, turning to rend, turning to overpower, to subdue, to conquer the vessel of life itself, creation's own embodiment. Had she not labored for aeons to give birth to a triumph of joy and beauty as fair as dawn, a creature of light to share the glowing consciousness of the whole, one of understanding as deep as her deeps are deep, of laughter as divine as tears and of tears as cleansing as laughter, one who was no alien to mercy, capable of new visions above predation, a familiar to the art of healing, above all a creature of tongues, creation itself no longer mute to express—to express—

What had gone wrong?"

Ecological speculative fiction of the highest order.

240 pages. 1985.
Paperback: $7.96